Animals of Australia

Dalmatian
KIDS

The DALMATIAN KIDS name and logo are trademarks of
Dalmatian Publishing Group, Atlanta, Georgia 30329.

Published by Dalmatian Kids, an imprint of Dalmatian Publishing Group.
Text Copyright © 2007 by Dalmatian Publishing Group, LLC
Art Copyright © 2007 Edizioni Larus S.p.A.

Printed in the U.S.A. • ISBN: 1-40373-241-8
07 08 09 B&M 9 8 7 6 5 4 3 2 1

Australia is filled with animals that are very, very different from those in other lands.

Millions of years ago, Australia was part of Asia, where three types of mammals lived: *monotremes*, which lay eggs; *marsupials*, which carry little ones in a pouch; and *placentals*, which grow babies inside their bodies.

When these animals came to Australia, they spread all over the continent. Kangaroos settled in the prairies, for example, wombats dug tunnels, and koalas took to the trees.

Animals of Australia

Sulfur-crested Cockatoo

Australian Pheasant

Marsupial Rat

Thorny Devil

Kangaroo

Cassowary

Koala

Wallaby

Tasmanian Devil

Echidna

Numbat

3

Koala

The koala looks like a teddy, but it's a marsupial—*not* a bear! This animal has a big head and body, a black nose, rounded ears with tufts of hair, and very strong toenails. Its chubby body, about 2½ feet high, is covered with soft, gray fur.

The koala lives quietly in the eucalyptus forest of eastern Australia, spending most of its time in the trees.

What does it eat?
Eucalyptus leaves—about two pound a day! The koala has a special intestine to help digest these poisonous leaves.

4

Joeys (Baby Koalas)

At birth, a joey weighs no more than an ounce—about the size of a lima bean! This newborn nurses for six months. Then, for a short time, it eats its mother's "pap," a mucuslike food that has bacteria to help the little koala eat poisonous eucalyptus leaves.

Did You Know?

The koala's pouch is turned upside down, unlike a kangaroo's. A joey has to hold on tight when its mother climbs around in the trees! Even after it can eat on its own, the mother koala watches her baby carefully.

Red Kangaroo

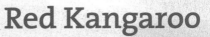

Red and gray kangaroos are the world's biggest marsupials. When the red kangaroo stands up, it's about 6½ feet tall! Males are reddish; females are grayer. Red kangaroos inhabit very dry areas. They live in small groups of two to ten, and follow adult males into green pastures to look for food.

What does it eat?
Plants, like fresh grass.

Joeys (Baby Kangaroos)

When a tiny joey is born, it does not look like a baby kangaroo. It is pink and hairless, and can't see. The fifth finger of its hand is already formed, however, and the baby has strong nails. So it grabs on to its mother's hair and climbs into her pouch.

The little one stays hidden there until it can walk and run. After 200 days, the baby kangaroo is covered with hair. Sometimes it leaves its mother's pouch, but the joey goes back when it's tired or afraid. As the joey grows larger, all four of its limbs may stick out as it snuggles into the pouch! By the time the baby weighs about 10 pounds, it can run very fast and leaves the pouch for good.

CREATURE FEATURE:

Male red kangaroos have very strong tails to fight with. A male spins on his tail and tries to hit an enemy in the stomach with his back feet. This heavy tail also helps the kangaroo to balance when he's hopping 6 feet high or running 20 mph.

Wallaby

The wallaby is a small kangaroo, about 3 feet tall with a 2½-foot tail. A crackerjack jumper, the wallaby moves easily between rocks, climbs steep walls, and creeps into deep spaces. This has earned him the name "Australian *chamois*" (goatlike antelope).

CREATURE FEATURE:
Chewing on hard roots wears down the wallaby's teeth until they fall out. These teeth are replaced by new ones!

Joeys (Baby Wallabies)

The female gives birth to one little wallaby, weighing about an ounce. It stays in its mother's pouch for about 200 days.

What does it eat?
Roots, buds, and grass.

Sugar Glider

A sugar glider is a marsupial that looks like a small gray opossum, with a black stripe from head to tail. It lives in the eucalyptus forest, but likes to hang out in the gardens of nearby houses.

A *membrane* (thin layer of tissue) connects this animal's hips to his feet. The membrane is called a glider.

When he's resting, the sugar glider stays folded up; but when he jumps off a tree, the membrane opens like a parachute, and he sails through the air! The sugar glider moves from one branch to another without ever touching the ground, where its predators live.

Baby Sugar Gliders

A baby sugar glider clings tightly to its mother, nursing on her milk. It also grabs her hair when the mother flies from tree to tree.

When a baby sugar glider grows up, he doesn't need to stay in his mother's pouch anymore, so he climbs onto his mother's back and just holds on!

Dingo

Dingoes are wild, wolflike dogs. A dingo stands 1½ feet high and weighs about 65 pounds. It has straight ears, a thick tail, and fur that is dark yellowish-tan to off-white.

Dingoes live in small family packs that *migrate* (move from place to place) every year, from central Australia to the coast. They are good hunters and tireless runners, known for traveling far.

What does it eat?
Animals of any size, like kangaroos, wallabies, wombats, sheep, and marsupial rats.

Baby Dingoes

Females make dens near waterways. In spring, they give birth to pups—about five to nine at a time. Baby dingoes are nursed on their mother's milk for about two months. Then, parents feed them prey that has been caught while hunting.

Pups leave the family when they are about five months old. Males join groups and hunt rabbits.

The baby dingoes' enemies are crocodiles, snakes, and eagles.

CREATURE FEATURE:
Dingoes don't bark. They howl, like wolves.

Did You Know?

Some 30,000 years ago, dingoes were not in Australia. Aborigines (native Australians) probably brought them over from Indonesia.

11

Platypus

The platypus is a very odd-looking creature! It has a strong body like an otter's, a beak like a duck's, stiff hair, and wide webbed feet. The platypus also has no teeth. Food is sucked into its mouth and then mashed.

This mammal lives in the currents of rivers and lakes in Australia and the island of Tasmania. It moves around through mud, sand, and rocks, coming up for air only every one to two minutes. It holds its prey in special sacks in its mouth.

The Baby Platypus

In late winter, the female digs a den at the end of a long tunnel, and lays three eggs. The babies are born hairless and blind.

For four months, they lick milk dripping from their mother's glands. Then the mother takes her little ones into the water to teach them to hunt for food.

What does it eat?
Small crustaceans, shrimp, crab, worms, snails, spiders, small fish, adult insects, or *larvae* (newly hatched insects).

Echidna

The back of the echidna, or spiny anteater, is completely covered with prickles! In case of danger, the echidna digs a hole and jumps in it, so only its prickles are showing.

An echidna's nails are very strong, and its long nose has two nostrils. This animal's sharp sense of smell makes up for its poor eyesight. It can sniff out prey from very far away! An echidna has no teeth. Its mouth has hard places, and when it draws in insects, it breaks them.

The echidna lives a *nocturnal* (nighttime) life in parts of Australia covered with plants.

Baby Echidnas

A baby echidna is called a puggle! A little puggle licks drops of milk that dribble from glands in its mother's belly. The baby stays in its mother's pouch until it grows prickles at about 10 weeks old. Then it hides in plants. The mother feeds her baby milk for about a year.

Did You Know?
The echidna can live to be 50 years old!

What does it eat?
Insects and worms, caught with its long snout, sticky tongue, and strong claws. Favorite foods are ants and termites.

Tasmanian Devil

The Tasmanian devil is brownish-black, with a short head and thick body. This fierce-looking creature, about the size of a small dog, is known for its spine-chilling screams and the bad odor it makes when it's afraid.

This marsupial used to be found all over Australia, but today it only lives on the island of Tasmania, just south of Australia. During the day, it rests in a den; at night, it hunts.

Baby Tasmanian Devils

Female Tasmanian devils can have as many as 30 pups at a time! However, only about four will survive.

After 15 weeks, newborns open their eyes. Because the babies are then too heavy to be carried in a pouch, the mother hides them in a hollow tree trunk, lined with leaves and grass. She nurses them until they are five months old, when they can catch insects and spiders on their own.

What does it eat?
Wallabies, kangaroo rats, birds, and lizards, as well as shrimp and fish.

CREATURE FEATURE:
The Tasmanian devil can run 12 miles without stopping!

Numbat

Numbat
Bilby
Wombat

The numbat is a brownish-gray, pouchless marsupial with light-colored stripes, a bushy tail, and pointed ears. It also has a long, sticky tongue that's good for catching insects.

   This small, gentle creature usually moves slowly but can trot up to 18 mph!

   The female has about four little ones in her den. Because she has no pouch, baby numbats hang on tightly to their mother's belly fur whenever she moves.

What does it eat?
Insects. The numbat gobbles up to 20,000 termites a day!

Bilby

The little bilby (about 1½ feet long) has a pointed face, soft, bluish-gray fur, and very long ears! This rabbitlike animal lives alone in dens about six feet deep. The secretive bilby marks its territory with scent and chases away any critters that come near.

   Young bilbies stay in their mother's pouch and nurse for up to 10 weeks.

What does it eat?
Insects, particularly termites.

Did You Know?
A bilby is also known as a bandicoot, a dalgyte, and a pinkie!

Wombat

The shy wombat, a "cousin" to the koala, has pointed ears and dense fur. It also has very strong nails that it uses to dig long, shallow tunnels leading to a large den. It lines its den with leaves and grass and likes to live there alone.

Baby Wombats

The mother wombat's pouch faces backward so her babies will be safe when she's digging a tunnel or moving around. As soon as little ones enter her pouch, they begin nursing.

What does it eat?
Grass, roots, leaves, and tree shoots.

Did You Know?
The wombat defends itself at home by blocking the den opening with its back—like a cork in a bottle! (Its back has a hard coat that's hard to claw.)

17

Johnston's Crocodile

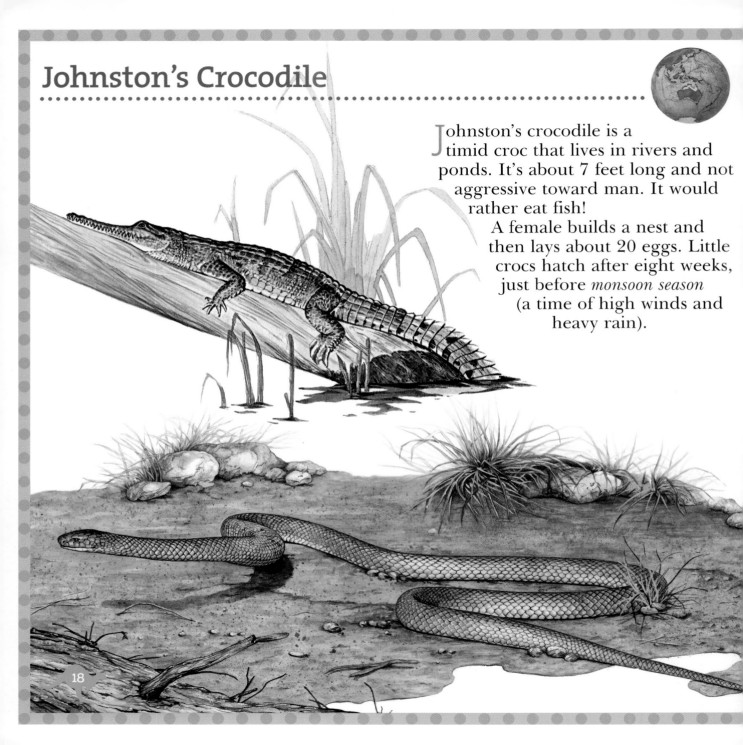

Johnston's crocodile is a timid croc that lives in rivers and ponds. It's about 7 feet long and not aggressive toward man. It would rather eat fish!

A female builds a nest and then lays about 20 eggs. Little crocs hatch after eight weeks, just before *monsoon season* (a time of high winds and heavy rain).

Frilled Lizard

This 2½-foot-long reptile is very quick. When the frilled lizard meets an enemy, it hisses, and a big, round frill opens around its neck, like an umbrella! This frill scares its enemy, and gives the lizard time to escape. It eats insects, spiders, small mammals, and birds' eggs.

King Brown Snake

Australia has more poisonous snakes than any other place on Earth. And the 9-foot-long king brown snake, or mulga, is one of the largest poisonous snakes in Australia.

A bite from the king brown snake is very dangerous. Its fangs are longer than an inch, and sink in deeply, so poison gets quickly into the victim!

Kookaburra

The kookaburra is a big bird about 18 inches long, with a huge body and a big head. It has a black bill, and its feathers are off-white with dark stripes.

The kookaburra lives in the forest and grassland. A very curious bird, it likes to visit house gardens!

Baby Kookaburras

Two to four chicks hatch in a nest in a hollowed-out tree trunk. Both parents protect the nest and defend the young against predators.

What does it eat?
Large insects, small mammals, birds, and lizards (even poisonous snakes!).

CREATURE FEATURE:
At sunrise, the kookaburra lets loose with a screechy, high-pitched "laugh" that wakes everybody up. Early colonists called the kookaburra an alarm clock!

Emu

The emu is a huge bird—6½ feet high and more than 100 pounds. It can't fly, but this big brown bird is an excellent runner. With the help of padded feet and three large toes, the emu can really zoom! It runs as fast as 30 mph.

Emus live in large flocks in the driest areas of Australia, but migrate in winter to the rainy coast for food.

In April, emus search for mates. After courting, the female digs a hole in the ground, lines it with grass and leaves, and lays up to 20 eggs. Then, for more than a month, the male takes care of the eggs. He never leaves the nest, and loses about 18 pounds! The eggs hatch in the rainy season.

What does it eat?
Leaves, grass, flowers, fruits, and seeds, as well as insects, like weevils.

Did You Know?
Emus like shiny objects. They will swallow keys, bottle caps, and money!

Cassowary

This big bird can grow to 5 or 6 feet tall. It is covered in feathers, but cannot fly. The cassowary's body is dark brown, with bright blue and red feathers growing in the folds of its neck.

If this bird or its young are in danger, it kicks at the enemy with its feet. (It can easily break a limb!) The cassowary is also a good jumper and swimmer.

What does it eat?
Grass, leaves, buds, fruit, bark, and seeds—as well as insects, worms, and shellfish.

Baby Cassowaries

The female builds a nest on land, carpeted with leaves. Then, she lays three to six big eggs. The male sits on the eggs to *incubate* them (keep them warm). After 50 days, the eggs hatch. Chicks have both light and dark feathers, so they can hide in the underbrush.

CREATURE FEATURE:
The helmetlike crest on the cassowary's head is used to push through underbrush.

Did You Know?

A cassowary's wings end in sharp prickles that protect him from rough underbrush, and predators.

Sulfur-crested Cockatoo

This cockatoo lives in forests and sometimes big city parks. It is intelligent and affectionate. It can imitate many sounds, including the human voice!

The sulfur-crested cockatoo scratches about the eucalyptus forests in search of buds, sprouts, leaves, plants, seeds, and fruit.

Did You Know?

Cockatoos are often kept as pets. They can live 40–50 years!

Galah
(Rose-breasted Cockatoo)

The galah has a lovely pink breast with a gray back. These birds often form enormous flocks that fly in a wave all over Australia and even into city parks. Both parents care for their young and are very affectionate with the newborns.